A Little About Me...

I've been living with Alpha-lady for around twenty years. I went through the initial twelve years attempting to discover the reason why I had these bizarre side effects. At long last, subsequent to asking to be tried, the finding returned as Alpha-lady. The allergist said to stay away from red meats and perhaps dairy. That sounded simple however wasn't just basic. I attempted to find more data online with very little achievement. I was appreciative to have a determination yet disappointed by the absence of information on clinical work force. My expectation is that I can help other people by sharing what I have realized throughout the long term. I have changed plans to make them Alpha-lady safe and will share a portion of those in this book. Much obliged to you to my loved ones for the love and backing all through this insane journey.

I additionally thank my Alpha-lady companions via online media gatherings. They have helped so many essentially by sharing their tales about tick illnesses including Alpha-lady. I have been supported and flabbergasted by their positivity.

Thank you for the valuable chance to impart data and plans to anybody ready to master, including loved ones of Alpha-lady positive people.

What is Alpha-gal Allergy Syndrome?

Alpha-lady Syndrome (AGS) is additionally called Alpha-lady sensitivity, red meat sensitivity, or tick chomp meat sensitivity. It is a significant, possibly dangerous hypersensitive reaction.

Alpha-lady is a sugar atom found in many vertebrates. It isn't ordinarily found in fish, reptiles, birds, or people.

That is pretty much all the web tells us. Alpha-lady just appears through a blood test. The skin prick test won't let you know if you have AGS.

Beware: Alpha-lady is likewise in items produced using well evolved creatures like beauty care products, cleansers, moisturizers, dairy, gelatin and medication.

Reactions can incorporate rash, hives, sickness, regurgitating, trouble breathing, drop in pulse, unsteadiness or faintness, extreme stomach torment, or gastrointestinal indications. These responses can be negligible or extreme. The normal response is accounted for to be between three to six hours after openness. The deferred response makes it more hard to analyze. Rage responses - also known as airborne allergens-have been accounted for in with regards to 33% of individuals with Alpha-lady. While smolder responses might take a brief period, it is for the most part promptly after exposure.

"Have an EpiPen with you at all times."

"You are honored in the event that you haven't encountered anaphylaxis."

Consistently conflicting might be the most ideal way to depict Alpha-lady. The greater part of us with AGS have had anaphylactic responses bringing about a visit to the trauma center. Teach your loved ones who might be giving you a ride to the clinic. You'll require a supporter to show the clinic staff. The greater part of them have never known about it. This is anything but an ordinary sensitivity and can't be treated in that capacity. I'm not a specialist and just talking from my experiences.

Anaphylaxis is a serious hypersensitive response and can effectsly affect the body.

*Dizziness *faintness *loss of cognizance *anxiety *shock *eye-swelling *itchy mouth *itchy throat *cough *hoarse voice *lips expanding *nasal blockage *difficulty breathing *wheezing, *shortness of breath *low circulatory strain * helpless course *low beat *chest torment *cramps *nausea
*vomiting * loose bowels *itchiness *hives *warmth *redness *rash *pale skin
*swelling in hands and feet.

"Are you exhausted simply perusing that list?"

Listen to your body. Unexplained torment could mean you are unconsciously presenting yourself to mammal.

"Data brings knowledge."

Keep two shots of epinephrine with you consistently. It just works for around twenty minutes. On the off chance that side effects return before you arrive at clinical assistance, another portion might be necessary.

Exercise is great for everybody… usually.

It is feasible to have practice prompted hypersensitivity. This appears to be normal with AGS patients. Try not to practice just subsequent to eating. Quit practicing quickly on the off chance that you notice any manifestations of hypersensitivity. I have consistently appreciated practicing and still do, however I needed to change the manner in which I get work out. In the event that I don't perspire - no response. There is a distinction in delicately sweating and really sweating.

Histamine is a compound made in the body that is delivered by white platelets into the circulatory system when the safe framework is guarding against a likely allergen. While receptor resistance fluctuates from one individual to another, keeping away from high receptor food varieties is useful for Alpha-lady positive individuals. It isn't not difficult to list all the high receptor food sources that might actually cause issues. Assuming it is aged, restored, or matured, limit your admission. Avoid additives. In addition to the fact that they are high in receptors, yet could incorporate warm blooded creature inferred ingredients.

"Set aside a few minutes for your health, so you will not possess to take energy for your illness."

Alpha-lady side effects and responses vary from one individual to another. "The most pessimistic scenario I've seen" is what my allergist told me. His speculation is that I invested an excess of energy without a finding and unwittingly was placing allergens into my body persistently. Facilitating more drifters (also known as ticks!) didn't help all things considered. My receptor pail topped off and flooded. Various indications followed including Bell's paralysis. I was in the eatery business dealing with food every day not understanding the significant issues that was causing. Cerebrum mist was terrible that I thought I suffered a heart attack and had been misdiagnosed with Bell's paralysis, that was before the AGS determination. We shut the eatery (a long-term privately-run company) and sold my kids' clothing store. My significant other kept cooking without me. Then I found out I had AGS. It was an extreme change with all we had as of now experienced, fortunately

I had a ton of help from loved ones. I lost a few companions in the process as well, but

that ended up being generally a good thing. Certain individuals failed to see the reason why I was unable to come to their social event assuming that they were barbecuing or making things like bean stew. I needed to focus on being sound, my dietary patterns and way of life needed to change. A course of grieving my previous lifestyle needed to happen for me to move on.

"Every section of life brings new blessings."

- **-Denial**... *no, I can't have a tick disease*
- **-Anger**... *how does a workaholic NOT work?*
- **-Bargaining...** *maybe God allowed this so I can educate people about tick diseases.*
- **-Depression...** *no one cares about tick diseases.*
- **-Acceptance...** *enjoy the little things.*

It required a very long time for me to acknowledge I can in any case appreciate life - slow student, I presume. Certain individuals move past AGS and some don't. Focus on what you can do rather than what you can't. Wake you up to a better approach for thinking and you'll see great blessings.

Restaurants are trying with AGS. You should have companions able to think twice about the determination of cafés. Continuously converse with the chief or gourmet expert with regards to cross-defilement. Assuming everything is cooked in a similar fryer or on a similar barbecue, it isn't protected. Places utilizing hamburger seasoning in their fryers are undependable. Try not to be hesitant to leave in the event that you don't have a good sense of security. There are foundations able to oblige you. Your loved ones love you and would prefer to change eateries as opposed to taking you to the trauma center in a couple hours.

"You are not a burden."

Normally, picking a fish café is a protected decision. An issue could emerge with cross-defilement or dairy. Pose inquiries for security, and consistently stress it's a genuine sensitivity - in addition to a narrow mindedness. Assuming you are a shrimp eater, know that a few nations infuse gelatin into shrimp. Gelatin is got from collagen taken from creature body parts. Schooling is vital. I love Mexican food. Cafés that serve it turned into an issue. Seethe responses from those steak fajitas sizzling through the air sent me into an asthma-like response. That is the point at which I understood smoke responses were genuine. I decided to begin going to my beloved eatery among lunch and dinner when they don't have an enormous group. The best table was at the rear of the bar, a long way from the kitchen. I might have quit going however settled on a choice to continue to partake in their food. They were exceptionally obliging to my necessities. Grill cafés with those incredible smelling smokers can now be an executioner assuming that you respond to exhaust. Veggie lover eateries might be a decent decision on the off chance that you're fine with no meat. Carrageenan is an added substance at times utilized in vegetarian items. It has a similar atomic construction as Alpha-lady. Exceptionally touchy individuals might respond to carrageenan. The body can remember it as Alpha-lady, the enemy.

"I'm in a real sense hypersensitive to
bull crap!"

I have frequently gone into an eatery with family or companions with the outlook they would have something protected on the menu. That isn't dependably the situation. I can't perceive you how often I needed to eat something from my reserve kept in my satchel while watching them eat food sources I once appreciated. I attempt to remind myself I'm there for the organization and can deal with it. "It's fine, you all eat." Sometimes I said that nearly tears. I began taking a refrigerator in my vehicle wherever I went loaded with a couple of things that would not make me wiped out. A few packaged waters even caused responses. Did you know hints of gelatin can be found in a few plastic jugs from organizations that utilization it in their purging cycle? I typically stay with unsweetened tea at cafés and utilize natural stevia for sugar. Assuming you go to a chain eatery, most have online allergen menus. That assists with dairy sensitivities however not hamburger or pork. Observing something marked veggie lover is protected the greater part of the time.

Unfortunately, it tends to be experimentation to sort out which eateries to visit. Many organizations send representatives to a class about food sensitivities and cross-defilement rehearses. The vast majority have no clue about AGS or even what creature is really a mammal.

"There are no mix-ups, just lessons."

Anxiety cautioning… The BEST choice is to set up your food in the security of your own home. It gets old preparing each supper for consistently, particularly when you don't feel better. Attempt to get ready more dinners on the great days and

freeze any extras for the not-super great days. Air fryers and moment pots are extraordinary once you figure out how to utilize them. Challenge you loved ones to assist with finding plans that are ok for you. Get innovative with replacements to your beloved plans so they can be Alpha-lady safe. It's a learning interaction that gets more straightforward as time passes by. My family was in the café business for ages, however there was still a ton of learning engaged with this better approach for cooking securely. Many stores offer natural things now which assists with shopping. It's ideal to utilize natural things sooner rather than later. A few brands of flavors have added substances that may not be protected. Sugar is brightened with bone burn, vertebrate obviously. Search for natural sugar or one that explicitly says 'bone burn free' on the bundling. Check fixing marks regularly. A few organizations change plans - I don't have the foggiest idea why. Living without additives is a lot better and more secure for everybody. At the point when you glance through the included plans, you'll perceive the way simple replacements can be.

> *"Nobody is conceived an extraordinary cook; one advances by doing."*

A sensitivity ready arm band or accessory can save your life. Focus on it to arrange one and consistently wear it. They can be redone. Mine says: Anaphylaxis, NO gelatin, NO dairy, NO warm blooded creature items, Alpha-lady Syndrome.

Keep as a main priority that prescriptions can contain vertebrate inferred fixings. My Alpha-lady companions encouraged me to change from Benadryl to Unisom Sleep Melts. They have a similar dynamic fixing, Diphenhydramine, however with less idle fixings like gelatin. I'm persuaded that Unisom Sleep Melts have held me back from utilizing my EpiPen commonly. They are fast dissolving, non-propensity framing and diminish queasiness. I never venture out from home without my EpiPen and Unisom Sleep Melts. Taking a couple of melts at the earliest hint of response will as a rule lighten indications. You might have to set down thereafter, yet it beats going to the trauma center. Continuously converse with your drug specialist about doctor prescribed medication. Chewable child ibuprofen works for my cerebral pains. Assuming you require something more grounded, really look at producers for buried fixings. Supportive data can be found via web-based media Alpha-lady pages. Individuals share data they have gotten from various organizations. Robert Woods Johnson Pharmacy at Rutgers

University is educated with regards to Alpha-lady safe drugs. They will help you, your primary care physician or pharmacist.
Phone number: 732-937-8842

Tick sicknesses have become normal in the United States and a few different nations. Some data can be found on the CDC site about the various sorts of ticks. You may not track down the whole truth on that site. It appears they minimize the reality of issues cause by tick sicknesses. Assuming an individual has one tick illness, usually another is stowing away in the circulation system. With any sickness, monitor everything that your body is saying to you. Many tick infections have comparable indications. Migraines, weariness, muscle hurts and joint torment are normal. A rheumatologist informed me I currently have joint pain probably brought about by the tick illness. Whoopee for me (embed sarcasm)!
It's normal to have rashes, fever/chills, and aversion to the sun. Tanning without becoming red and splotchy is by all accounts over for me. I love the ocean side yet am exceptionally mindful with regards to sun openness now. That is something else those parasitic drifters attempted to take from me. I actually partake in the ocean side for get-aways yet keep an umbrella close by. Terrible ticks can't remove my delight of being holiday with my family. Ticks love me such a lot of that they free-tumble from trees just to have a dinner with me - on me. A great many people with tick illnesses love to be outside. That is the reason we get to meet so many of the undesirable guests.

"Ticks are small scale, genuine vampires!"

Prevention...

This is something for every individual to discover how functions for them that Treats cause a response. Rejuvenating oils have functioned admirably for me. I utilize a brand named Doterra. There are many brands, and I'm not advancing this one. I needed to tell you the brand I use since I'm posting their ingredients.

Tick Repellent

40 drops of

Terrashield 10 drops

of lemongrass 10

drops of eucalyptus 4

ounces of water

Put into a splash jug and shake well. Shower onto garments prior to partaking in your open air exercises. I likewise softly fog my legs when wearing shorts.

Stores generally stock tick anti-agents, or you can arrange on the web. Continuously check elements for something that might cause a response. Once again, the smartest choice will be something labeled vegan. Try not to quit setting up camp or appreciating open air exercises on the grounds that a parasitic animal is
lurking.

"Take in the outside air and have fun."

Since having responses to numerous drugs, I have gleaned some significant knowledge about regular solutions for sicknesses. By and by, I'm just sharing my encounters. You might not disapprove of any of the medication you are taking. I felt it was too exorbitant to even consider utilizing a compound drug store - in addition to it implied heading to a major city which made me feel awkward. I love my medicinal oils. In the event that I have a cerebral pain, I put a drop of peppermint on my finger and rub into my sanctuaries. Try not to get it in your eyes since it will burn.

Anxiety Oil

In a 10 ml roller bottle,

add: 10 drops of

peppermint

10 drops of lavender

10 drops of frankincense

Add a transporter oil to fill the jug I use grapeseed

Rub onto wrist each day and each evening. The way in to this working is being unwavering in applying day by day. Now and then I sniff lavender in the event that I feel overpowered. It has a quieting effect.

Diffusers swirl around with new aromas. I utilize various aromas as per how I feel at the time.

"... 1031 references to medicinal balms in the Bible."

You can arrange splash containers and roller bottles on the web. Amazon is my decision. I would rather not advance them either, yet it's a reality. They make it simple to arrange and get things quickly.

Did you realize that insects, mice and other vermin disdain the smell of peppermint? You can put some on cotton balls and spot them around the house. You can likewise add around 15 drops to a water container and splash around the house. That is superior to utilizing compound splashes and taking a risk of having a reaction.

I regularly add ten drops of peppermint rejuvenating ointment and ten drops of eucalyptus medicinal oil to my diffuser. As it courses through the air, I feel like I can inhale further. Doterra has made a blend of oils explicitly to advance profound relaxing. It's just named Breathe.

Painful Joints Blend

In a 10 ml roller bottle,

add: 8 drops of eucalyptus

oil

10 drops of peppermint

oil 12 drops of lavender

oil

Add transporter oil to fill the container - olive oil will

work Gently rub agonizing regions two times a day.

If you do a quest for medicinal balm mixes, you will see a few decisions. I pick the mixes that utilization the most un-number of oils and afterward check whether it works. This makes the blending system simpler and sets aside cash. There are additionally mixes for better rest, pulse balance, stomach related assistance, and even antiperspirant. I incorporated the mixes I use frequently for your data. I don't miss my nervousness mix or everybody appears to take note. Having Alpha-lady provoked me to find out with regards to elective medicines that I have figured out how to love.

Cannabidiol (CBD) oil is an item that is gotten from marijuana. It's a sort of cannabinoid, which are the synthetic substances normally found in pot plants. Despite the fact that it comes from maryjane plants, CBD doesn't make a 'high' impact or any type of inebriation that is brought about by another cannabinoid, known as THC. Assuming that you will attempt CBD oil, do the examination. Track down an organization that sells an unadulterated structure without added substances. It might cost somewhat more however doesn't need as much day by day. I'm not burning through cash on solutions like I was previously, so I have a decent outlook on purchasing CBD oil. At the point when I began taking the unadulterated structure consistently, the thing that matters was astonishing. I have less agony, better rest, and not as worn out during the day. Fatigue from coincidental openness went from three days to only one day.

"Wellbeing isn't esteemed until ailment comes."

Acupuncture is a type of elective medication. Despite the fact that it is disputable, I need to give as much data as possible from my encounters. I have had one treatment now - an extraordinary treatment. While there is no solution for Alpha-lady, certain individuals have further developed utilizing Soliman's Auricular Allergy Treatment otherwise called SAAT. It is said to 'reconstruct' your safe framework to stop by responding to allergens. Dr. Nader Soliman, a trailblazer in auricular needle therapy, finished long stretches of clinical review on a great many sensitivity victims. Through his refined strategy for SAAT, people presently experience extreme decrease and even end of sensitivity manifestations. This treatment is being utilized on AGS patients with some achievement. After one treatment (a little needle set decisively in the ear for quite some time), I can eat cheddar with practically no torment or response. My objective - to have the option to have cheddar again and improve cross defilement. That was refined alongside less smoke responses. I have had hypersensitivity too often to at any point need red meats once more, however certain individuals have had accomplishment with that as well. I started to feel mostly ordinary once more. After certain ticks dropped out of trees while I was picnicking - and obviously had a cookout with my blood, some cross defilement issues returned. I anticipate another SAAT visit.

When cooking at home…

Alpha-lady amicable food varieties can be subbed in numerous plans to make protected and pleasant dinners. Purchasing new food sources is best yet unimaginable all of the time. When

purchasing canned items, ensure they are natural. Frozen vegetables normally have no added substances which makes them safe. Bundled meats can have additives, so attempt to pick the ones with few fixings and NO additives. A few organizations add fillers to flavors - consistently look at them for those undesirable added substances. I comprehend it's occasionally hard to track down natural food varieties in modest communities. I attempt to go through basic fixings and stock when I track down canned natural vegetables. I have made plans or gotten them from companions and on the web. When you understand what you can substitute, you'll see most plans can be changed. Estimating isn't a good time for me since I go by taste as I add flavors. The accompanying plans might should be changed as you would prefer. Subsequent to having Bell's paralysis multiple times, once in a while I have an issue tasting salt. Subsequent to disposing of all warm blooded animal, no more Bell's paralysis except for super durable harm was finished. Useless vocal line and synkinesis cause a few issues - as yet living and appreciating life though.

"The mystery of progress is to concentrate all your energy, not on battling the old, but rather on building the new."   Socrates

Substitutions:

1 tbsp cornstarch = 2 tbsp unbleached flour

1 cup buttermilk =add 1 tbsp vinegar to 1 c. *almond milk*

1 cup cream, harsh or weighty = ⅓ cup plant margarine with ⅔ cup non-dairy milk

1 tbsp minced onion = 1 little new onion

⅛ tsp garlic powder = 1 little squeezed clove of garlic

3 medium bananas = 1 cup mashed

Butter = plant butter

Milk = non-dairy milk

Flour = unbleached flour or almond flour for gluten-free
Ketchup = natural ketchup

Chocolate = non-dairy dim chocolate (search for Enjoy Life products)

Sugar = natural or bone-burn free sugar; stevia

Bacon = turkey bacon or chicken bacon

Pork frankfurter = duck or turkey sausage

Cheeses = non-dairy choices or dietary yeast

"Put resources into a meat thermometer for safety."

Appetizers

And

Dips

VEGAN CHEESE SAUCE

- *½ cup nutritional yeast*
- *⅓ cup all-purpose unbleached*
- *flour 1 tsp sea salt*
- *2 cups cold water*
- *¼ cup plant*
- *butter 1 tsp*
  mustard

Whisk together nourishing yeast, unbleached flour, and ocean salt in a dish. Put on burner, medium hotness and rush in the water. Heat to the point of boiling, decrease hotness and cook for 1 moment. Keep rushing to hold it back from adhering to the skillet. Eliminate from hotness and mix in plant spread and mustard. This makes an incredible messy tasting sauce to pour over dishes that require cheddar. On the off chance that excessively slender, add flour. In the event that excessively thick, add 1 tbsp water or almond milk.

To make into cheddar plunge, add ½ tbsp garlic powder and 1 tbsp stew powder. More salt and slashed jalapenos are optional.

"Grin and say CHEESE please."

HOMEMADE SALSA

- *15 ounce can organic petite diced tomatoes or use 3 fresh medium sized tomatoes and chop to petite size*

- *1 cup finely chopped chili peppers*
- *½ cup finely chopped onions*
- *1 tsp garlic powder*
- *½ tsp cumin*
- *½ tsp bone-char free sugar*
- *½ tsp sea salt*
- *1 finely chopped jalapeno (optional)*

Mix all fixings together in a huge bowl and utilize a blender to mix. You can utilize a food processor or blender, however be mindful so as not to over-mix assuming that you like the thick sort of salsa. Present with chips and enjoy!

*Tomatoes are high in receptor so keep away from assuming you've had an unfavorably susceptible response recently.

"Salsa... a bite or a dance. Why not pick both?"

CARROT DIP

- *4 medium carrots*
- *2 tbsp olive oil*
- *½ tsp sea salt*
- *3 tsp sesame seeds*
- *½ tsp black pepper*
- *1 garlic clove*
- *½ cup water*

Peel and clean carrots, bubble until delicate. Cut into 1" pieces. In a food processor or the hard way, grind carrots adding all fixings until you have a glue like consistency. Serve at room temperature with pita chips.

PALEO SAUSAGE BALLS

- *1 lb duck or turkey sausage*
- *1 cup plus 2 tbsp almond flour*
- *3 tbsp tapioca starch*
- *3 tbsp nutritional yeast*
- *1 tsp sea salt*
- *¼ tsp black pepper*
- *2 tsp thyme leaves*
- *1 tsp ground sage*
- *2 eggs*
- *¼ tsp cayenne (optional)*

Preheat stove 400° F. Line baking sheet with material paper. In an enormous blending bowl, consolidate frankfurter, flour, starch, yeast and flavors. Overlap in eggs, mix well until completely consolidated. Scoop out little balls forming them with your hands. Place on baking sheet equitably divided. Heat 30 to 35 minutes or until completely cooked.

"Paleo plans mean Alpha-lady safe? - Not always."

BLACK BEAN DIP

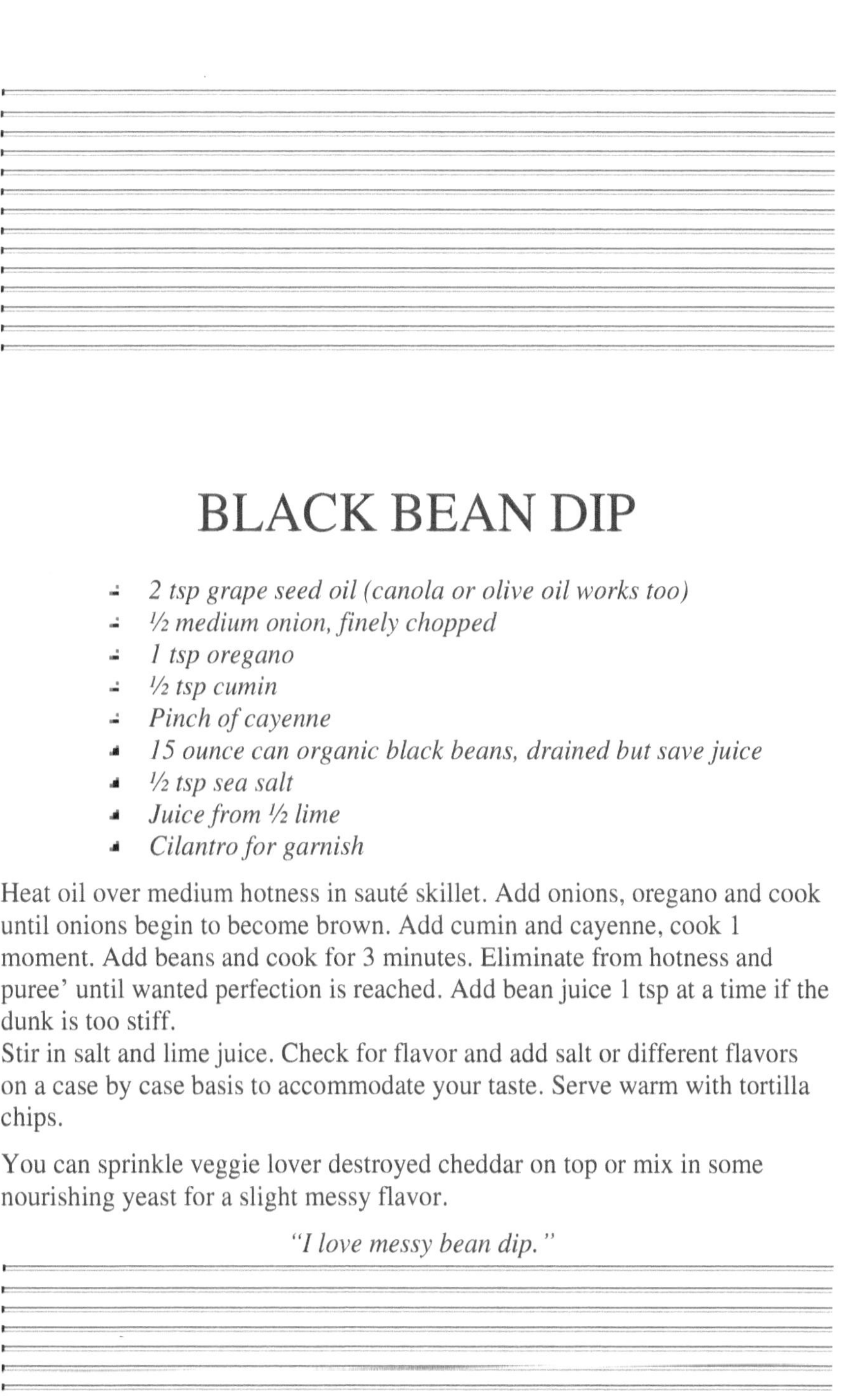

- *2 tsp grape seed oil (canola or olive oil works too)*
- *½ medium onion, finely chopped*
- *1 tsp oregano*
- *½ tsp cumin*
- *Pinch of cayenne*
- *15 ounce can organic black beans, drained but save juice*
- *½ tsp sea salt*
- *Juice from ½ lime*
- *Cilantro for garnish*

Heat oil over medium hotness in sauté skillet. Add onions, oregano and cook until onions begin to become brown. Add cumin and cayenne, cook 1 moment. Add beans and cook for 3 minutes. Eliminate from hotness and puree' until wanted perfection is reached. Add bean juice 1 tsp at a time if the dunk is too stiff.

Stir in salt and lime juice. Check for flavor and add salt or different flavors on a case by case basis to accommodate your taste. Serve warm with tortilla chips.

You can sprinkle veggie lover destroyed cheddar on top or mix in some nourishing yeast for a slight messy flavor.

"I love messy bean dip."

AVOCADO DIP

- *2 ripe avocados*
- *½ tsp garlic powder*
- *¼ tsp sea salt*
- *⅛ tsp black pepper*
- *¼ onion finely chopped*
- *¼ chopped tomato (optional)*
- *1 lime*

Peel the avocados and eliminate seed. Place into a bowl, add garlic powder, salt, pepper, onion, and tomato. Tenderly pound all fixings together. Mix in the lime juice and it's prepared to eat. Present with chips or use for a garnish on your cherished Mexican dish.

Make a serving of mixed greens and utilize this for your dressing. You can thin the avocado dunk by blending in 1 tbsp softened plant margarine and 1 tbsp non-dairy milk.

"Avocados are loaded with sound, gainful fats that assist you with feeling full and satisfied."

ARTICHOKE DIP

- *8 ounces artichokes cut up*
- *1 cup mayonnaise (I prefer Dukes)*
- *¼ tsp garlic powder (2 cloves garlic)*
- *1 cup shredded vegan parmesan cheese*

Preheat broiler to 350° F. Combine as one all fixings. Heat for 25 minutes. Present with tortilla chips or pita chips.

"Artichokes are known similar to a superfood on account of their undeniable degrees of cell reinforcements. Concentrates on show they assist with adjusting pulse, lower cholesterol and can further develop liver function."

↑That's amazing!

COWBOY CAVIAR

- *15 ounce can of black-eyed peas, drained (another option is to cook a bag of frozen black-eyed peas, cooked and cooled)*
- *15 ounce can of corn, drained (optional to use frozen bag of corn)*
- *1 ¾ cup olive oil*
- *¾ cup vinegar*
- *1 small onion, finely chopped*

- *½ cup diced tomatoes*
- *¼ cup diced*
- *jalapenos 1 tbsp*
- *garlic powder 1 tbsp oregano*
- *1 tbsp crushed red*
- *pepper 2 tsp lemon juice*

Mix flavors and fluids, shake well. Add to the excess fixings and mix. Chill and present with chips or crackers.

"This is great filled in as a side plate of mixed greens too."

VEGGIE DIP

- *24 ounces roasted red peppers*
- *½ tsp garlic powder*
- *2 tsp mustard*
- *⅛ tsp sea salt*
- *⅛ tsp black pepper*
- *1 medium yellow pepper, diced*
- *1 tbsp ginger root, minced*
- *¼ cup basil (fresh) chopped*

Use a blender or food processor, consolidate broiled peppers, garlic, ginger root and mustard. Puree' until smooth. Season to taste with salt and pepper. Transfer to a huge bowl and crease in leftover ingredients.

*Homemade cooked peppers - preheat stove to 450° F. Slice the peppers down the middle, eliminate stems, seeds and films. Lay the peppers on a *foil-lined baking sheet cut side down. Broil the peppers for 15-20 minutes or until skins are dull and have imploded. Eliminate from broiler. Skin should fall off effectively now. Dispose of skin, hack, dice or freeze for use.*

"Natively constructed is the best!"

Soups

&

Salads

BANANA APPLE SALAD

- *⅓ cup honey*
- *½ tsp lemon zest 3*
- *tbsp lemon juice*
- *¼ tsp sea salt*
- *1 tsp ground ginger*
- *⅛ tsp nutmeg*
- *1 lb bananas, cut into ½ inch slices 1*
- *lb apples, cut into ½ inch chunks*
- *Chopped nuts (optional)*

In an enormous bowl, whisk together honey, zing, juice, salt, ginger and nutmeg. Add bananas and apples, throw and serve.

"An invigorating summer side or lunch."

ENGLISH PEA SALAD

- *15 ounces cooked sweet green peas*
- *½ medium onion, finely*
- *chopped 2 boiled eggs, chopped*
- *1 cup sweet pickles, chopped*
- *½ tsp sea salt*
- *¼ tsp black pepper*

- *2 green onions, chopped*
- *½ cup mayonnaise (Dukes is my choice)*

Let the peas cool. Put all fixings in a bowl and blend well. Chill for somewhere around one hour before serving.

"Attempt it… assuming you like it, make it for loved ones. Individuals will request your recipe."

BROCCOLI SALAD

- *1 head broccoli*
- *1 small bag shredded carrots*
- *½ cup raisins*
- *1 cup mayonnaise (prefer Dukes)*
- *¼ cup bone-char free sugar*
- *2 tbsp vinegar*
- *½ cup chopped red onions*
- *¼ cup chopped walnuts*
- *¼ cup chopped pineapple (optional)*

Cut broccoli into scaled down pieces and put in a huge bowl. Add carrots, raisins, mayo, sugar, vinegar, and onions. Blend well. Top with pecans and enjoy.

*I just utilize natural products of the soil. It is better to avoid additives and pesticides. My throat got irritated, and I would hack prior to changing to natural only.

"Broccoli… loaded with nutrients and does a body good."

CHICKEN SALAD

- *2 cooked chicken breasts, diced*
- *¼ cup mayonnaise (can add more according to your taste) 1*
- *small peeled and chopped organic apple*
- *¼ onion, chopped (optional)*
- *¼ cup chopped grapes*
- *Splash of lemon juice*
- *½ tsp mustard*
- *Sea salt and pepper to taste*

Mix all fixings together in a medium measured bowl.

Dip-present with Alpha-lady safe crackers

Sandwich-layer on bread (I use Dave's Killer Bread), add lettuce and tomato

Wrap-put on a tortilla with a leaf of lettuce

Salad-place on top of a bed of greens like romaine and spinach

Lettuce Wrap-roll in a romaine lettuce leaf

"Bliss is having great food to take to the picnic."

MACARONI SALAD

- *1 cup uncooked elbow macaroni*
- *½ cup mayonnaise*
- *2 hardboiled eggs, chopped*
- *1 green pepper, chopped*
- *1 cucumber, chopped*
- *1 medium onion, chopped*

Cook elbow macaroni as coordinated on the bundle. Channel and add remaining fixings. Mix delicately and chill.

"Pasta servings of mixed greens are an extraordinary option to cookouts."

PASTA E FAGIOLO SOUP

- *1 tbsp olive oil*
- *1 lb ground chicken or ground*
- *turkey 2 organic carrots, diced*
- *2 stalks organic celery,*
- *diced 1 medium onion,*
  diced
- *28 ounces crushed tomatoes (prefer*
- *organic) 2 bay leaves*
- *1 tbsp oregano*
- *½ tsp thyme*
- *1 tsp sea*
  salt
- *½ tsp black pepper*
- *2 cans white or pinto beans (or make them from*
- *scratch) 1 cup elbow macaroni*

Add oil, onion and meat to enormous pot and brown. Add different fixings with the exception of pasta. Stew on oven something like 60 minutes. Cook pasta as indicated by the bundle and add to soup.

*Crock pot-earthy colored meat the equivalent yet add to sLow cooker with fixings aside from pasta. High for 3 hours. Low

for 6 hours. Add pasta throughout the previous thirty minutes to permit time for it to cook in the container pot.

CHICKEN SUMMER STEW

- *2 boneless chicken*
- *breasts 1 tsp sea salt*
- *½ tsp black pepper*
- *1 tbsp unbleached*
- *flour 2 tbsp olive oil*
- *1 ½ cups yellow*
- *corn 3 tbsp plant butter*
- *1 yellow squash, sliced*
- *thinly 1 small zucchini, sliced thinly*
- *10 ounces frozen baby lima beans, thawed*
- *3 ripe plum tomatoes, seeded and cut into ⅓ inch*
- *dice 4 cups organic chicken broth*
- *¼ cup fresh chives- ½ inch length*

Season chicken with salt and pepper. Sprinkle with flour. Heat olive oil in a 2 ½ quart skillet over medium hotness. Add chicken; Cook covered until chicken is finished. Eliminate from heat, place chicken on a board to cool. Soften spread in container; add squash, zucchini, lima beans, and corn. Cook, blending frequently, until squash is withered for around 4-5 minutes. Cut chicken into ¾ inch lumps. Add to

vegetables in addition to tomatoes and stock. Season with salt and pepper. Cook until warmed through-3 to 4 minutes. Sprinkle chives on top before serving.

HOMEMADE CHILI

- *1 lb ground chicken or ground turkey 1*
- *tbsp olive oil*
- *1 small onion chopped 1*
- *tsp sea salt*
- *½ black pepper*
- *1 tbsp garlic powder 2*
- *tbsp chili powder*
- *Add 3 cans tri-blend organic beans or use homemade pinto beans*
- *1 can organic tomato sauce 1*
- *tbsp bone-char free sugar*

In a huge pot, add oil, meat and hacked onion. As the meat tans, mix in the salt, pepper, garlic and stew powder. When the meat is done, add beans, pureed tomatoes and sugar. Stew for 30 minutes to 60 minutes, adding water if excessively thick. Add more flavors as indicated by your taste.

"Relax and partake in that chili!"

CHICKEN VEGGIE SOUP

- *1 lb ground chicken or ground*
- *turkey 1 tbsp olive oil*
- *½ onion, chopped*
- *16 ounces (one bag) frozen vegetable*
- *2 potatoes, cleaned and cut in 1-inch chunks*

- *1 can organic petite diced tomatoes or wash and dice one small tomato*
- *1 lb organic chicken bone*
- *broth 2 tsp sea salt*
- *1 tsp black pepper*
- *½ tbsp garlic*
- *powder 1 tbsp oregano*

Add oil, onion and meat to an enormous pot. As the meat earthy colors, add ocean salt, pepper, garlic and oregano. At the point when the meat is done, add bone stock, frozen vegetables, potatoes, and diced tomatoes. Bring to a boil, then lower heat to simmer for about 30-45 minutes. More stock or water can be added assuming that you lean toward more slender soup.

"Do your squats, eat your veggies and be kind."

Main
Dishes

MEATLOAF STUFFED
BELL PEPPERS

1 lb ground chicken or ground turkey
¼ cup crushed crackers

¼ cup organic ketchup (plus 4 tbsp optional) 1
egg, beaten
¼ tsp onion powder 1
tsp garlic powder 1 tsp
sea salt
½ tsp black pepper
*4 bell peppers with tops removed and seeds discarded (when choosing peppers, look for
the ones with the flattest bottom.)*

Preheat stove 350° F. In a huge blending bowl, consolidate the meat,
saltines, ¼ cup of ketchup, egg, onion powder, garlic powder, salt and
pepper. Blend completely. Partition the meat blend equally among the
peppers. Heat for 50 minutes. Remove from broiler and add a tbsp of
ketchup on every one. This progression can be skipped assuming you
incline toward meatloaf without garnish. Set back into stove for an
additional 10 minutes. Utilize a meat thermometer to ensure the interior
temperature has arrived at 165° F. Cool marginally and serve.

"Meatloaf with ketchup is yummy, yet 'great sauce' works too"

TURKEY TENDERLOIN

- *2 lb package of turkey tenderloins (there should be 2 in the package)*
- *2 tbsp olive*
- *oil 1 tsp sea salt*
- *2 tbsp oregano*
- *½ tsp mustard*
- *1 tbsp thyme (optional)*
- *½ tsp black pepper*
- *1 tbsp garlic powder*

Preheat broiler to 400° F. Place turkey tenderloin in a broiler safe container with sides
- fixing the dish with foil will save money on tidy up. Score tenderloins across the top with a blade, so the oil and flavors can saturate the meat. Place a tbsp of oil on every flank. Rub flavors into every tenderloin. Cover with foil and heat for around 60 minutes. Eliminate the foil covering the midsections and check for interior temperature of 165°. Over cooking can make the meat be dry, so you might need to actually take a look at them about ¾ way through cooking time. Allow the midsections to cool for around 10 minutes before cutting. These are like pork midsections however no pork.

BARBEQUE CHICKEN

- *4- 4 ounce boneless chicken breasts, dark meat can be used with a little added cooking time*

- *8 ounces organic barbeque sauce*

Instant Pot-Lay the chicken bosoms in the pot. Cover chicken with grill sauce, seal the top. Utilize the 'meat' button and cook for 28 minutes. Subsequent to delivering the air, open and shred the meat utilizing two forks. Serve

Crock Pot-Put the chicken bosoms in the slow cooker, cover with sauce. Cook on high for 2 hours or low for 4 hours. Shred the chicken and serve.

BBQ chicken can be served on buns (I use Dave's Killer Bread). Additional sauce can be added by your taste. Making BBQ spuds is another choice. Simply heat a potato, add a tbsp of plant margarine, chicken, more sauce whenever wanted and destroyed veggie lover cheese.

Homemade Barbeque Sauce

- *8 ounces organic ketchup*
- *2 tsp chili powder*
- *2 tsp garlic powder 1 tsp onion powder 2 tsp organic sugar*

Mix all fixings and change in accordance with your taste.

"Satisfaction is homemade."

TACO MEAT

- *1 lb ground chicken or ground turkey*
- *1 small onion, chopped*
- *½ tbsp garlic powder*
- *1 tbsp chili powder*
- *1 tsp sea salt*
- *½ tsp black pepper*
- *1 tbsp olive oil*
- *¼ cup of water*

Add oil, meat and cleaved onions to skillet. Go to medium hotness, add any remaining fixings aside from the water. At the point when meat looks done, go down to a stew and add water. Let stew until the water has reduced. Taste to check whether you favor more flavors. I frequently add some additional stew powder and garlic. It just requirements to stew on low for around ten minutes, making a speedy and simple meal.

*Add to taco shells, top with lettuce, vegetarian cheddar and tomatoes. Utilize a flour tortilla for delicate tacos. *Put on a bed of lettuce for a taco salad, top with natural salsa. *Spread some tortilla chips on a plate, add taco meat, lettuce and veggie lover cheddar. (Vegetarian cheddar sauce is great with this also.)

"Taco preparing mix can be made ahead and kept in shaker or fixed in a baggie. Substitute 1 tsp onion powder instead of the little onion. I like genuine onions for the smell while cooking."

APPLE TURKEY CHOPS

- *4 turkey breast cutlets*
- *2 medium apples, peeled, cored and sliced*
- *2 tsp plant butter*
- *¼ tsp cinnamon (optional)*
- *Sea salt and pepper to taste*

Preheat stove to 350° F. Salt and pepper cutlets on the two sides. Brown the cutlets in a skillet. Place sautéed culets in gently lubed baking dish. Layer apples on top of cutlets. Spot with plant margarine and sprinkle with cinnamon.

Cover and prepare until apples and cutlets are finished. Check following 20 minutes to check whether interior temperature has arrived at 165° F. Stoves differ, and may require additional cooking time.

LEMON BAKED CHICKEN

- *4 boneless skinless chicken breasts (dark meat can be used with added cooking time*
- *¼ cup plus 2 tbsp lemon juice*
- *½ cup melted plant*
- *butter 1 tsp garlic*
- *1 tsp*
- *oregano 1*
  tsp sea salt
- *½ tsp black pepper*

Preheat stove to 350° F. Place chicken in a softly lubed baking dish. Join all fixings, pour over chicken, heat covered for 30 minutes. Eliminate from stove. Uncover and spoon juices over the chicken. Get back to stove for an additional 15 minutes. Eliminate from stove and actually look at inward temperature. It ought to be essentially 165° F. Prepare longer in the event that the temperature has not arrived at that point. Baking occasions differ as indicated by the size of the chicken breasts.

"Chicken or egg-which came first?"

SMOTHERED CHICKEN

- *4 boneless skinless chicken breasts*
- *½ cup unbleached*
- *flour 2 tbsp olive oil*
- *½ onion, chopped*
- *½ tbsp chili powder*
- *½ tbsp garlic*
- *powder 1 tsp sea salt*
- *½ tsp black pepper*

In a profound skillet add olive oil and cleaved onion, put on medium hotness on oven. Add the flavors to the flour and spread out on a plate. Flour the chicken bosoms on the two sides and add to the skillet. Ensure you can noticeably see the oil in the skillet. On the off chance that not, add an additional a tbsp. The leftover flour left on the plate can now be added to the skillet too. Attempt to place it around the chicken into the oil. Cook chicken on one side for about 5 minutes, then flip to the other side for another 5 minutes. Then add water to just cover the chicken.

Let it come to a boil, then cover and simmer for about 30 minutes, stirring the gravy around chicken occasionally. Actually take a look at the sauce for taste and add more flavors on a case by case basis for your inclination. The chicken ought to be delicate now. Add more water in the event that the sauce is excessively thick. Assuming that it's slender, you might need to allow it to stew a little longer.

Anything with sauce is viewed as antiquated solace food. Made pureed potatoes or rice to put with covered chicken since you have sauce prepared to serve.

SPAGHETTI MEAT SAUCE

- *1 lb ground chicken or ground turkey*
- *½ onion,*
- *chopped 1 tbsp*
  olive oil
- *1 can organic tomato sauce*
- *1 can organic petite diced tomatoes*
- *½ tbsp garlic*
- *powder 1 tbsp*
  oregano
- *1 tsp sea salt*
- *½ tsp black pepper*
- *1 tbsp bone-char free sugar*

In a profound skillet, add olive oil, onion and meat. Cook over medium hotness until done. Add every excess fixing. Bring the sauce to a boil, then simmer for 20-30 minutes, stirring occasionally. My family loves some additional garlic and oregano, yet consistently season to your favored taste. It very well may be diminished by adding water.

When purchasing pasta, really take a look at the fixings on the bundle for added additives. Attempt to purchase pasta with minimal measure of fixings. I like to purchase natural, yet it's quite difficult all the time to find.

MEXICAN LASAGNA

- *1 lb ground chicken or ground turkey 1*
- *small onion chopped*
- *2 tbsp olive oil*
- *1 tbsp garlic powder 1*
- *½ tbsp chili powder 1*
- *tsp sea salt*
- *½ tsp black pepper 12*
- *corn tortillas*
- *1 can organic corn, drained (frozen can be used)*
- *1 can organic tri-blend beans (homemade pinto beans can be used instead) 1*
- *can organic petite diced tomatoes*
- *6 ounces shredded vegan cheese or vegan cheese sauce*

Preheat broiler to 350° F.

In a profound skillet, add 1 tbsp olive oil and hacked onion to meat. Earthy colored meat blending the onions into the meat. Add garlic, stew powder. Salt and pepper. Mix in corn, beans and tomatoes. Bring to a boil, then remove from heat. In a baking dish, spread 1 tbsp oil on base. Layer 6 corn tortillas in the base. Scoop a large portion of the meat combination onto the tortillas. Layer the other 6 tortillas, then add the rest of the meat mixture. Put destroyed cheddar or cheddar sauce on top. Heat for 30-40 minutes. Eliminate from broiler, let cool somewhat before cutting.

Sweets

And

Other

Things

OLD FASHIONED HOMEMADE BISCUITS

- *2 cups unbleached all purpose flour (make it gluten-free by substituting almond flour)*
- *2 ½ tsp baking powder (most brands are safe, but always check ingredients label)*
- *½ tsp sea salt*
- *⅓ cup all vegetable shortening*
- *¾ cup unsweetened almond*
- *milk 1 tbsp softened plant butter*

Preheat stove to 475° F. In a medium combining bowl mix as one flour, baking powder and salt. Cut in shortening until it looks like coarse pieces. (A baked good blender makes it simpler however excessive.) Make a well in the focal point of the flour combination. Add milk. Utilizing a fork, mix until dampened and batter pulls from the sides of the bowl (mixture will be tacky). On a floured surface, delicately ply batter with floured hands until almost smooth. Roll batter to ¾ inch thickness. Cut batter with a 2 ½ inch roll shaper (I utilize a glass) dunking shaper into flour between cuts. Place rolls near one another on a delicately lubed baking sheet. Brush tops with delicate spread. Prepare 12-15 minutes or until focus is finished. Yields around 8 rolls. Add plant spread, honey or an all-organic product jam. (Much appreciated sister Vicky for instructing me.)

"Practice makes perfect."

CHOCOLATE GRAVY

- *¾ cup bone-char free sugar*
- *½ cup unbleached all-purpose flour*
- *⅓ cup cocoa*
- *3 cups unsweetened almond milk 1*
- *tsp vanilla*
- *½ stick plant butter*
- *½ cup warm water*

Mix dry fixings together. Add warm water and mix well. Heat almond milk in pan until bubbling. Empty the hot almond milk into the cocoa combination, mixing continually until it begins to thicken. Add plant spread and vanilla. The key is mixing continually, and it will end up incredible. What about having this with those antiquated custom made biscuits.

"Chocolate comes from cocoa which is a tree. That makes it a plant.
Chocolate is salad."

APPLE CRISP

- *4 cups peeled and slice*
- *apples 1 tsp cinnamon*
- *¼ to ½ tsp sea salt*

- *¾ cup unbleached all-purpose flour*
- *¼ cup water*
- *1 cup bone-char free sugar*
- *⅓ cup plant butter*

Preheat stove to 350° F.

Spread apples in buttered baking dish. Sprinkle with cinnamon and salt. Add water equitably to apples (don't mix). Combine as one flour, sugar, and margarine until combination looks brittle. Drop combination over apples. Heat for 40 minutes.
Serve warm.

MICROWAVE MUG CAKE

- *¼ cup unbleached all-purpose flour*
- *¼ cup bone-char free*
- *sugar 2 tbsp cocoa powder*
- *Pinch of salt*
- *Pinch of baking*
- *soda 1 tbsp water*
- *2 tbsp olive oil*

- *3 tbsp unsweetened almond*
- *milk A splash of vanilla*

In a huge espresso cup, put every one of the dry fixings and mix. Then, at that point, add water, oil, milk and vanilla. Mix well. Microwave for 2 minutes. Then, at that point, let cool for 2 minutes.

This is extremely sweet, however assuming you truly have a sweet tooth… you can punch holes in it and pour chocolate syrup over it. There's one chocolate syrup that says 'Essentially Five' on it and just holds back five ingredients.

"This mug cake serves one individual and is a unique treat."

SUGAR COOKIES

- *1 cup plant butter*
- *1 cup bone-char free*
- *sugar 1 large egg*
- *1 tbsp vanilla*
- *¼ tsp almond extract (optional)*
- *2 ½ cups unbleached all-purpose flour*
- *½ tsp baking soda*
- *½ tsp baking powder*

Topping: ½ cup bone-singe free sugar, for moving treat mixture balls

Preheat stove to 350° F.

In an enormous blending bowl, cream together spread and sugar until light and cushioned. Add egg, concentrates, and blend until smooth. Add flour, baking powder, baking pop, and blend until just joined to a treat mixture consistency. Scoop out little divides of the mixture and make balls. Roll in the sugar (beating). Place them on a treat sheet, fixed with material paper. Heat for 12 minutes or until edges are softly brilliant. Permit to cool and enjoy!

"This is my better half's favorite!"

PEANUT BUTTER FUDGE

- *3 ½ cups organic powdered sugar*
- *1 stick plant butter*
- *½ cup peanut butter (Earth Balance is my choice)*
- *¼ cup unsweetened almond milk*
- *1 tsp vanilla*

Pour sugar into huge microwave safe bowl. Add margarine, milk and peanut butter. Try not to mix. Place in microwave for 2 ½ minutes or until margarine liquefies. Remove bowl from microwave, add vanilla and blend in with electric blender. Fill a 8 x 8-inch baking dish that has been fixed with foil. Place in cooler for 15 minutes.

Sometimes stickiness causes issues with thickening. This is as yet flavorful regardless of whether it make a thick fudge.

HOT COCOA

- *¼ cup cocoa*
- *½ cup bone-char free*
- *sugar Dash of sea salt*
- *⅓ cup hot water*
- *1 quart (32 ounces) unsweetened almond milk*
- *¾ tsp vanilla*

Add cocoa, sugar, salt and boiling water to a pot. Heat to the point of boiling and mix for 2 minutes. Add milk. Mix and hotness. TRY NOT TO BOIL. Eliminate from heat and add

¾ tsp vanilla. Whisk or use blender until frothy. Put into mugs and

appreciate! You can add vegetarian marshmallows or sans dairy whipped

cream to the top.

BEST VEGAN BROWNIES

- *2 tbsp ground flaxseed*
- *6 tbsp water or chilled brewed coffee*
- *1 cup dairy-free chocolate chips, melted*
- *1 cup bone-char free sugar*
- *6 tbsp plant butter*
- *1 tsp vanilla*
- *¾ cup + 2 tbsp unbleached all-purpose flour (can substitute gluten-free flour)*
- *1 tsp sea salt*
- *1 tsp baking powder*
- *¼ cup cocoa powder*
- *1 ½ cups dairy-free chocolate chips*

Preheat broiler to 350° F. Consolidate flaxseed and water (or espresso). Allow it to sit for 10 minutes, to frame a gel. Line a square skillet with material paper and put away. In an enormous blending bowl, add margarine and sugar, whisk well. Include the flaxseed combination, liquefied chocolate, vanilla and blend well, until shiny. Presently mix in flour, baking powder, salt and cocoa powder until consolidated. Don't overmix. Crease in the 1 ½ cups of chocolate chips. Move brownie hitter into the lined container. Prepare for 30-35 minutes.

Remove brownies from stove and cool totally prior to cutting into 12 pieces. You can not tell these are veggie lover. They are delicious.

"Brownies are my most loved dessert!"

MICROWAVE BURGER BUN

- *3 tbsp almond flour or unbleached all-purpose flour*
- *½ tsp baking*
- *powder 1 ½ tbsp olive oil*
- *1 egg*
- *Pinch of sea salt*
- *Pinch of nutritional yeast flakes*

In a little oat bowl (microwave-safe bowl), completely blend the baking powder and flour guaranteeing there are no clusters. Add the oil, egg, salt and yeast, blend well. Utilizing a fork, ensure it is blended well in with no bunches. Microwave on high for 90 seconds. At the point when you remove from the microwave, the bun will be looking like the lower part of the bowl. Allow it to cool prior to cutting. This can be toasted for turkey burgers or emu burgers. It can likewise be utilized for egg sandwiches or similarly as a bun with your meal.

This formula makes one serving.

"Turkey burgers are charming, yet emu burgers help me to remember those antiquated meat burgers."

There are a lot more plans I might have included. Here are a few clues.

Instead of hamburger, use emu meat. The ground emu is best with duck fat as it is exceptionally lean meat. Emu posterior can be utilized instead of hamburger broil. Emu filets will make great steaks, cooked as you did meat steaks.

Remember your cherished pork hack plans? Supplant pork slashes with turkey cutlets. They can be barbecued, covered with sauce, singed or prepared. Pork midsection plans can in any case be followed just by subbing turkey tenderloin.

Any ground hamburger formula can be trailed by subbing ground turkey, ground chicken or ground emu. Add 1 tbsp oil for each pound of ground meat.

Turkey bacon can be utilized instead of pork bacon for cooking. When making a 'bacon' sandwich or an egg and bacon sandwich, I use Al Fresco uncured chicken bacon completely cooked. I additionally add it to green beans for some extra zing. The completely cooked chicken bacon (2 pieces) can be placed into microwave for 20 seconds, let set a couple of moments for crispness.

Although I did exclude any fish plans, we frequently eat barbecued fish.

FISH

For fish around 2 inches thick, season with your beloved flavors. Be certain the barbecue is perfect. Apply some olive oil to a paper towel. Utilizing utensils, rub the oil covered paper towel along the meshes. Let the temperature of the barbecue heat up between 550° to 600° F. Lay the fish skin side down onto the mesh. Try not to attempt to move or flip fish until singed great as an afterthought down on the barbecue. Cook about 6 minutes on one side lid down, then turn for about 6 minutes on the other side with lid down. The fish should turn out flaky and delicious.

Fish enveloped by foil and barbecued is likewise simple and tastes incredible. Lay the fish in the foil, add wanted flavors and a sprinkle of olive oil. Add a cut of lemon on every one. Overlay up edges of foil so that it's totally fixed, making a tent. (I have likewise included cut squash or zucchini the highest point of the fish to cook alongside the fish.) It's ideal to cook foil wrapped food sources on backhanded hotness, which means don't put on direct fire. Heat a large portion of the barbecue at high hotness. Put the foil bundles on the other half, close barbecue and cook around 15 minutes. The steam made inside the foil tent prepares this supper flawlessly. Change cooking time as per the thickness of the fish. Foil bundles can be steamed in a 400° stove on the off chance that climate isn't great for barbecuing outside.

Things I learned the hard way…

Who might have figured alpha-lady would in any case be available on warm blooded creature items on the off chance that the creature is dead?

Do not lick an envelope to seal it. Manifestations for me were prompt with tongue getting numb and enlarging. The envelopes that seal without licking them are the best choice.

Check your gauzes prior to applying to your skin. The tenacity can be vertebrate based causing redness and a rash. Trouble breathing was additionally one of my symptoms.

Monitor leads from a heart screen wound up in excruciating consuming subsequent to being on the skin for about 60 minutes. The skin under the leads was red with small

rankles. The arrangement was involving leads for delicate skin. Make certain to request these assuming you want to go to the clinic or crisis room.

Scotch tape… they make a plant-based tape now.

Suede boots worn over socks and stockings… this I was unable to accept and wore them a subsequent time. That demonstrated the initial time wasn't only an accident. My feet and advantages to the highest point of the boot line tingled seriously and became red. No more softened cowhide boots for me. Some gripe about calfskin furniture however I haven't encountered that.

My head tingled for around three weeks. I at last requested that a companion check out my scalp. She was stunned to see it was covered with red checks and seemed like somebody had torn my head everywhere. I quickly different to a guaranteed veggie lover cleanser. Recuperating started and issue solved.

Face lotion was publicized as veggie lover. I got it and attempted it. My face and neck became hot and red. I began perspiring moreover. I checked out the compartment. It didn't have a confirmed veggie lover image anyplace. Despite the fact that it was publicized as veggie lover, it was not.

Hotel sheets can be washed in any sort of cleanser. Subsequent to encountering rash and trouble breathing, we just travel in our own camper with all my safe items.

Ant nibbles currently cause hypersensitivity. I stepped in a bed of subterranean insects and got a few nibbles on my foot and lower leg. Quickly irritation, redness and enlarging began. Inside a few hours, I had cerebrum mist, depletion, pulse drop and sickness. Manifestations were ceaselessly deteriorating, so I took Unisom Sleep Melts and set down. Subsequent to resting for around ten hours, I woke up to knocks and irritation where the chomps were and still felt exceptionally drained. Different side effects were better, yet it was extremely intense working that day (which was the day after the bites).

Others have announced being adversely affected by honey bee or potentially wasp stings after the analysis of Alpha-lady. Fortunately, I have not been stung. After additional review, it appears subterranean insects and honey bees are hereditarily related. Since I realize insect chomps cause a response, it's a good idea that honey bees would too.

Driving or riding in a vehicle. Out of nowhere there's that dead skunk smell. Without understanding a response could happen from that, I went into an asthma attack.
This

occurred time and again. *Continuously keep your cooling vents on inside air.* It may not shut down all conceivable smoke responses out yet will help.

Ice cream made with almond milk caused responses multiple times before I understood it contained carrageenan. *Veggie lover doesn't dependably mean safe.*

Deodorant can be awful, causing underarm impulsive and consuming. Search for a veggie lover antiperspirant that will work for you. Everybody is distinctive on this one.

I needed to supplant my toothpaste. Gracious my, and the toothbrush with tongue cleaner on the back caused me to feel like I had been eating razor blades.

Be cautious with regards to utilizing extremely sharp steels with lanolin. There's nothing similar to consuming torment all around the shaved regions. I utilized natural coconut oil to help. The customary coconut oil made it worse!

A message from my husband...

"Alpha-lady is not kidding. Continuously be a promoter for your cherished one and accept they are harming and conceivably discouraged. Life might need to change for the whole family and that is alright. Loved ones need to acknowledge things are diverse to help. This can get genuine quick. What may not cause a response one time will be hypersensitivity the following time. I saw her up in the center of the late evening heaving a larger number of occasions than you can envision. Be encouraging even when it's difficult and you've had a rough day. I've watched what my better half has experienced and how much reading up it took for her to figure out how to live with this infection. She's seen numerous experts just to discover every one of the things she was going through must be connected with Alpha-lady. Her PCP needed a second assessment because of her numerous indications. We

went to Memphis two times to see a hypersensitivity subject matter expert, just to be told to find something agreeable to do at home and avoid swarms. He was unable to clarify her big numbers with every one of the insurances she was at that point taking. We love to go in our RV and appreciate life while keeping her safe. Experience consistently without limit. Be steady. Remain safe."